QUEEN'S GATE
JUNIOR SCHOOL

Queen's Gate Junior School
133 Queen's Gate
London SW7 5LF
071-589 3587

WEIRD AND WONDERFUL INSECTS

SUE HADDEN

WEIRD AND
WONDERFUL

BIRDS
FISH
FROGS AND TOADS
INSECTS
SNAKES
SPIDERS

Cover: A mantis nymph mimicking a flower.

Editor: Geraldine Purcell
Designer: Bruce Low

First published in 1991 by Wayland (Publishers) Limited
61 Western Road, Hove, East Sussex BN3 1JD, England

British Library Cataloguing in Publication Data
Hadden, Sue
Weird and wonderful insects
(Weird and wonderful)
I. Title   II. Series
595.7

ISBN 0–7502–0175–4

Typeset by Kalligraphic Design Ltd, Horley, Surrey
Printed and bound in Italy by L.E.G.O. S.p.A., Vicenza

CONTENTS

1. Great and small   4

2. Odd bodies and strange faces   7

3. Changing shape   8

4. On the move   11

5. Home sweet home   12

6. Food stores   15

7. Insect assassins   16

8. Hide and seek   19

9. Leave me alone!   20

10. Pretenders   23

11. Fierce and fearless   24

12. Courtship signals   27

13. Parasites and partners   28

GLOSSARY   30

FURTHER READING   31

INDEX   32

1. Great and small

There are at least 750,000 different **species** of insect in the world. Some scientists think there may be over 10 million species. With so many different kinds of insects, it is not surprising that they come in all shapes and sizes.

You would soon know if a goliath beetle landed close to you! This flying, giant African beetle is the heaviest in the world, weighing up to 100 g. Goliath beetles are very long too, measuring about 15 cm.

Such large flying insects may look frightening, but they are harmless fruit-eating insects.

Some insects are so small that you need to use a magnifying glass to see them properly. Springtails are tiny insects, often just 1 mm long. Different kinds of springtails live in different places. Look carefully in the soil or among leaf litter, around ponds or the seashore and you may just spot one of these mini-beasts.

Below This goliath beetle is almost as big as the banana it is eating.

Right A group of freshwater springtails on the surface of a pond.

2. Odd bodies and strange faces

This violin beetle from the forests of Indonesia is certainly one of the more oddly-shaped insects. Its body flaps make it look like a violin, but the flaps are really designed to help the beetle to blend in with the pattern of a tree fungus. Although the violin beetle has a very odd-looking body, it has the same features which most insects have. It has six legs, a pair of **antennae** and a body divided into three sections: the head, the **thorax** and the **abdomen**.

The lantern bug from southeast Asia and South America has a very strange face because it has an amazing 'false' head. No one is sure why the bug has a head shaped like this but it is probably to scare away its enemies. Lantern bugs may look fierce, but they are harmless and feed on sap (juices) from plants and trees. They are called lantern bugs because people used to believe that the large, 'false' head glowed in the dark, like a lantern, but this is not true.

Left Its long neck and round body have given the violin beetle its name.

Below Its odd-looking 'false' head makes the lantern bug look very scary.

3. Changing shape

Insects hatch from eggs and then go through a series of amazing body-changing stages, called **metamorphosis**. After hatching most insects become a **larva** and then a **pupa** before they reach their final adult body form.

A ladybird larva hatches out of an egg in early summer. The larva must eat as much as it can so that its body has plenty of energy to turn into a pupa. The larva's body slowly changes shape while in its tight pupal skin. After many months it emerges from the pupa as an adult ladybird, with new wings, ready to fly off.

Some insect larvae look similar to the adult. A damselfly larva (called a nymph) lives underwater in ponds. It sheds its skin each time its body gets bigger. Gradually the nymph grows wings, and its body and legs grow longer. When it is ready to become an adult, the nymph crawls out of its pond, on to a plant's stalk. Within about two hours, the nymph's skin has split and a beautiful new damselfly emerges.

Below When ladybirds come out of their pupal skin, they do not have spots.

Right A damselfly pushing itself out of its old larval skin.

4. On the move

Some insects have amazing ways of travelling, whether it is in the air or over water.

A cockchafer beetle has to work hard to lift its heavy body and sturdy legs off the ground. To get airborne, the chafer must pump plenty of air into air sacs (pockets) in its body.

Cockchafers are noisy, clumsy flyers and on fine summer evenings they often fly into people's homes and zoom around the lights. But, although they keep bumping into objects and falling to the floor, these heavyweight beetles rarely hurt themselves.

Left A cockchafer in flight. You can see its clear wings and wing cases.

The water measurer walks around on the surfaces of ponds and lakes. How does it do this without sinking? Well, this member of the bug family is very lightweight. It uses its long legs to spread its weight evenly across the water surface. Also, the water measurer is supported by the thin but very strong film formed by the water surface. This is called the surface tension. The water measurer rests on the surface, waiting for an insect to fall into the pond. The water measurer then moves across the water and quickly stabs its **prey** with its sharp mouthparts.

Below A water measurer resting on the surface of a pond.

5.   Home sweet home

Insects live in a wide variety of places – underground, in trees or in and around water.

Some spend their entire lives under water, like the water scorpion. It stays below the water surface and when an insect or a small fish passes by, the water scorpion seizes it with its pincer-like front legs. Water scorpions can stay under water because they have a special breathing tube, like a snorkel. It sticks out of the water and brings air down to the water scorpion still in the pond.

Weaver ants have an unusual way of making a home – they sew one! The ants live in the **tropical** forests of Africa, southeast Asia and Australia, so they can find plenty of leaves. First of all a line of worker ants pulls two leaves together. Then they sew them up with sticky strands of silk produced from the ant larvae. To do this, other worker ants each hold a larva in their jaws and move the larvae from one side to the other, like a needle and thread. The finished nest is a snug ball of leaves.

Below A larva is being used to help the weaver ants glue a nest together.

Right You can see the water scorpion's air tube reaching to the water's surface.

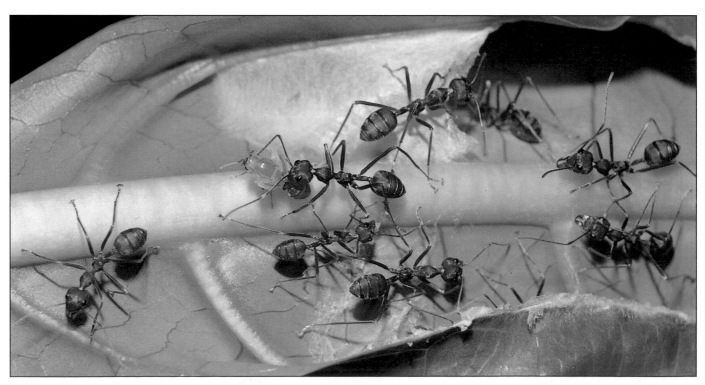

6. Food stores

Some insects must work hard to have enough food and drink, and they have clever ways of making sure they have enough to eat all year round.

Honeypot ants live in the Australian desert. During the very short rainy season, the ants feed on **nectar** from desert flowers. But in the long dry season the flowers cannot grow and the ants could go hungry. However, they survive by using some worker ants as honey stores. During the rainy season, these 'storage' ants are constantly fed with nectar and water until their abdomens swell up like balloons! They store enough honey to feed the whole ant **colony** until the flowers bloom again.

Darkling beetles live in the hot, dry Namib desert of southern Africa. The only moisture there comes from mist that drifts in off the Atlantic Ocean. The mist is too fine to drink but it slowly **condenses** into water droplets when it touches the darkling beetle's body. Then the beetle tilts up its body and the droplets run down the grooves on its back, into its thirsty mouth.

Left This honeypot ant is used as a store for honey for the ant colony.

Below A darkling beetle in its dry desert home.

7. Insect assassins

Many insects hunt other insects for food. They use some very clever tricks for catching their prey.

One of the fiercest hunters is the praying mantis. This strange-looking insect lives in warm parts of the world, especially tropical countries. The mantis waits under a flower or a leaf, keeping very still, so that it is hard to see. When an insect comes to feed, the mantis seizes it with its razor-sharp claws. Its victim cannot escape and will be eaten alive.

Assassin bugs are also fierce insect-eaters. They are armed with sharp, piercing mouthparts. Once the assassin bug has seized an insect in its forelegs, it injects poison to stop its prey from struggling. Then the bug uses its sharp mouth-tube to suck the blood out of its prey.

Below An assassin bug, from Central America, feeding on its prey.

Right Mantids are fierce hunters and sometimes they even eat each other.

8. Hide and seek

Many insects are **camouflaged** either to avoid being eaten or to hide so that they can catch their prey by surprise.

Flower mantids are coloured white, pink or green to blend in with tropical flowers. Some have legs shaped like flat, flower petals. When a flower mantis sits still on the type of flower it is camouflaged with, the mantis is perfectly disguised. Any insect or small bird coming to visit the beautiful flower for nectar has a nasty surprise in store!

Cleverly disguised insects called thorn bugs use their camouflage to protect themselves from **predators**. They stay as a group, all facing in one direction, on a plant's stem. The bugs keep very still, so that predators, such as birds, are fooled into thinking that they are just thorns on a stem. In this way the thorn bugs usually avoid being eaten.

Left When hunting, this flower mantis hides among white tropical flowers.

Below These thorn bugs look like rows of thorns on a stem.

9. Leave me alone!

Insects often use colour and patterns to warn predators to keep away. Nature uses three colours as warning signals: red, yellow and black. Birds and other animals have learned that insects coloured like this are poisonous, or at least taste unpleasant.

The **caterpillars** of the cinnabar moth are poisonous and their yellow and black stripes warn birds not to eat them. Adult cinnabar moths have red and black wings, showing that they too are poisonous. Warning colours are also used in insects with powerful stings. This is why bees and wasps have yellow and black stripes.

Patterns on insects also have a purpose. The io moth from the USA has a pair of large spots on its hind wings. They look just like staring eyes. The moth does not usually show its 'eyes' when it is resting. But if a bird or other predator comes near, the io moth flashes its eyespots and flies off. The big eyes may frighten the bird or at least confuse it for a moment, giving the moth time to escape.

Below An io moth shows its large eye spots to warn off an enemy.

Right Poisonous cinnabar moths are coloured red and black.

10. Pretenders

Not all insects are what they seem. The hornet moth has a very clever disguise. With its yellow stripes and clear, narrow wings, the moth fools its predators into believing it is a dangerous hornet. The only clues that give the moth away are that it has thicker legs than a wasp and the antennae of a moth. But birds are none the wiser and most predators leave well alone, so this moth enjoys a peaceful life.

Birds keep well away from some angry ants, which can squirt acid from their tails. So a type of harmless tropical treehopper has developed a fantastic disguise as an ant. Its abdomen, legs and wings all blend in with the leaf it sits on. From a distance, only the black ant marking on its thorax shows up. Predators avoid the 'ant' and the treehopper is safe. What a brilliant trick for an unarmed bug!

Left This 'hornet' would not sting you because it is really a hornet moth.

Below A predator would be fooled by this treehopper's disguise as an ant.

11.   Fierce and fearless

Caterpillars usually rely on good camouflage or on sharp spines to protect them from being eaten. But one caterpillar defends itself in an amazing way.

The fierce-looking puss moth caterpillar rears up at an enemy, lashing out with its whip-like tail streamers. To look more frightening, the caterpillar draws in its head to show a bright red patch and false eyes. Sometimes it squirts strong acid at the enemy, just like ants do. This startling display scares away most predators. Afterwards, when it is no longer in danger, the caterpillar returns to looking quite normal and harmless.

Male stag beetles fight over the right to **mate** with a female. They have a wrestling match using their huge, powerful jaws, which look like a pair of antlers, as weapons. A large male stag beetle can easily throw another male around, gripping him in his pincer-like jaws. The loser gets thrown to the ground. Because of his strength the winner of the battle is more likely to attract the female to mate with him.

Below Two male stag beetles in an impressive wrestling match.

Right A puss moth caterpillar looks very fierce when in its warning display.

12. Courtship signals

Colours are used by many insects during **courtship** to attract a mate.

Most moths fly and mate at night and therefore tend not to be so colourful. But one of the most beautiful and colourful moths in the world is the *Urania leilus* moth from South America. It flies during the day, so it needs bright colours to attract a mate. The beautiful colours on the wings are produced by scales which catch the sunlight as the moth flies. A mate will be able to see these bright, shimmering colours and will be attracted to the moth.

Male and female glow-worms attract each other at night with flashes of bright green light. The light comes from a special **organ** in their tails. A male glow-worm follows the much brighter flashes sent out by a female, until he finds her and then mates with her. Glow-worms are not really worms, as you may think from the name, but members of the beetle family.

Left A glow-worm flashing light from its tail is signalling that it is ready to mate.

Below This day-time flying moth has shimmering colours to attract a mate.

13. Parasites and partners

Poisonous tarantula spiders have little to fear from insects, except for the tarantula hawk wasp. The female hawk wasp attacks the dangerous tarantula with a vicious sting. When she has managed to sting the spider, it is **paralyzed**. While the tarantula cannot move, the female hawk wasp drags it into a burrow and lays an egg on it.

Later, the egg will hatch into a wasp larva and it will begin to eat the tarantula. The spider cannot do anything to stop this and is slowly eaten alive. The wasp larva is a **parasite**, living off the spider and giving it nothing in return.

Sometimes two very different insect species can live together and each gain some reward. For example, ants are known to look after a group of greenfly, or aphids. The aphids produce a delicious sweet liquid called honeydew, which the ants like to feed on. So the ants 'milk' the honeydew from the aphids. As a kind of payment for this food source, the ants help to protect the aphids from predators, such as ladybirds.

Below A tarantula hawk wasp has caught its victim and will soon lay an egg on the spider.

Right An ant drinking honeydew from some aphids. Their 'partnership' works well.

GLOSSARY

Abdomen The lower part of an insect's body. Inside are its heart, digestive system and organs for producing young.

Antennae The pair of feelers on an insect's head.

Camouflaged Coloured or patterned to blend in with the background.

Caterpillar The pupal stage of a butterfly or moth.

Colony A group of ants living and working together.

Condenses Changes from water vapour (mist or steam) into water droplets.

Courtship The time when males and females of a species attract each other before they mate.

Larva The first stage of an insect which hatches from an egg. Sometimes called a grub.

Mate The act which males and females of a species perform in order to reproduce.

Metamorphosis The series of changes that an insect goes through from a larva to adult.

Nectar The sugary substance produced by flowers.

Organ A part of the body that performs a particular function, such as the heart.

Paralyzed Unable to move.

Parasite An animal (often an insect) which lives and feeds on another animal.

Predators Animals that hunt other animals for food.

Prey An animal that is hunted and eaten by another animal.

Pupa The stage in an insect's life when the larva slowly changes into the adult insect. The pupa seems to be resting in a tight skin, but in fact all kinds of changes are happening to its body.

Species A particular kind of animal that is different from all other kinds. Only members of the same species can reproduce together.

Thorax The part of an insect's body below its head. The thorax is divided into three segments, each with a pair of legs. Wings are also attached to the thorax.

Tropical The very warm parts of the world that lie between two imaginary lines around the Earth we call the Tropic of Cancer and the Tropic of Capricorn.

FURTHER READING

Discovering Ants, Christopher O'Toole
  (Wayland, 1986)
Discovering Bugs, George McGavin
  (Wayland, 1988)
Discovering Butterflies and Moths,
  Keith Porter (Wayland, 1986)
*Discovering Damselflies and
  Dragonflies*, Linda Losito (Wayland,
  1987)
Insect (Eyewitness series), Laurence
  Mound (Dorling Kindersley, 1990)
Mysteries and Marvels of Insect Life,
  Jennifer Owen (Usborne, 1984)
Poisonous Insects (First Sight series),
  Lionel Bender (Franklin Watts, 1988)

Picture Acknowledgements

Ardea London Ltd/I R Beames 25, J Mason 22; Bruce Coleman Ltd/J & D Bartlett 4,
J Burton 8, A Compost 12, K Taylor 10, 11, 15, 21; Frank Lane Pictures/B Borrell 17,
Hoflinger 29; NHPA/A Bannister COVER, S Dalton 19, 24, O Rogge 14, M W F Tweedie 27;
Oxford Scientific Films Ltd/G I Bernard 5, R Blythe 26, J A L Cooke 23, P Devries 7, 16,
M Fogden 28, R Jackman 13, Mantis Wildlife Films 6, J Robinson 20; Papilio/18;
Planet Earth Pictures/W Harris 9.

INDEX

Numbers in **bold** indicate photographs.

Abdomen 7, 23
Africa 4, 12, 15
Ant 28, **29**
Antennae 7, 23
Aphids 28, **29**
Asia 7, 12
Assassin bug 16, **16**
Atlantic Ocean 15
Australia 12, 15

Bees 20

Camouflage 19
Caterpillars 20, 24
Cinnabar moth 20, **21**
Cockchafer beetle **10**, 11
Courtship 27

Damselfly nymph 8, **9**
Darkling beetle 15, **15**

Flower mantids **18**, 19

Glow-worms **26**, 27
Goliath beetle 4, **4**

Honeypot ants **14**, 15
Hornet moth **22**, 23

Indonesia 7
Io moths 20, **20**

Ladybird larva 8, **8**

Lantern bugs 7, **7**
Larva 8

Metamorphosis 8

Namib desert (Africa) 15

Praying mantids 16, **17**
Predators 23
Prey 11
Pupa 8
Puss moth caterpillar 24, **25**

South America 7
Springtails 4, **5**
Stag beetles 24, **24**

Tarantula hawk wasp 28, **28**
Thorax 7
Thorn bugs 19, **19**
Treehoppers 23, **23**

Urania leilus moth 27, **27**
USA 20

Violin (fiddle) beetle **6**, 7

Weaver ants 12, **12**
Warning
    colours 20
    displays 24
Wasps 20, 28
Water measurer 11, **11**
Water scorpion 12, **13**